DATE DUE			

31329000516258

920
J
Joseph, Paul.

Backstreet Boys

YOUNG PROFILES

Backstreet Boys

Paul Joseph

ABDO Publishing Company

visit us at
www.abdopub.com

Published by ABDO Publishing Company, 4940 Viking Drive, Edina, Minnesota 55435.
Copyright © 1999 by Abdo Consulting Group, Inc. International copyrights reserved in
all countries. No part of this book may be reproduced in any form without written
permission from the publisher.

Printed in the United States.

Photo credits: AP/Wide World; Shooting Star
Edited by Tamara L. Britton, K.M. Brielmaier

Library of Congress Cataloging-in-Publication Data

Joseph, Paul, 1970-
    Backstreet Boys / Paul Joseph.
        p. cm. -- (Young profiles)
    Includes index.
    Summary: A biography of the singing group from Orlando, Florida, that
achieved international fame before making it big in the United States.
    ISBN 1-57765-350-5 (hardcover)
    ISBN 1-57765-352-1 (paperback)
    1. Backstreet Boys--Juvenile literature. 2. Singers--United States--Biography--
Juvenile literature.   [1. Backstreet Boys. 2. Bands (Music)]. I. Title. II. Series.
ML3930.B203J67   1999
782.42166'092'2--dc21
    [B]   99-31788
                                                  CIP

Contents

The Backstreet Boys

When people think of Orlando, Florida, they may think of Disney World or Universal Studios. But now they also think of the Backstreet Boys. A.J. McLean, Howie Dorough, Nick Carter, Brian Littrell, and Kevin Richardson form the music group known as the Backstreet Boys.

The Backstreet Boys formed in Orlando, and they have taken over the world with their wonderful **vocals** and unbelievable dancing. People all over the world rush out to buy their albums and see them perform live.

Opposite page: The Backstreet Boys take a break from their hectic tour of Europe.

The Backstreet Boys are one of today's hottest bands. But fame didn't happen overnight. It all started in Orlando—at Disney World! With a little luck and a lot of work the talented boys came together to become bigger and better than any of them had ever dreamed.

Profile of the Backstreet Boys

Kevin

Full Name: Kevin Scott Richardson

Nickname: Train

Birthday: October 3, 1972

Birthplace: Lexington, Kentucky

Instruments: Keyboards, bass, **vocals**

Favorite Musicians: R. Kelly, Babyface, The Artist

Favorite Television Show: *Roseanne*

Favorite Sports: Waterskiing, basketball, hockey

Favorite Color: Royal Blue

Favorite Food: Asian

Pets: A cat named Quincy

6

Howie

Full Name: Howard Dwaine Dorough

Nickname: Howie D

Birthday: August 22, 1973

Birthplace: Orlando, Florida

Instruments: Guitar, **vocals**

Favorite Musicians: Jon Secada, Bobby Brown

Favorite Television Show: *Seinfeld*

Favorite Sports: Waterskiing, racquetball

Favorite Color: Purple

Favorite Food: Asian

Pets: None

Brian

Full Name: Brian Thomas Littrell

Nickname: B-Rok

Birthday: February 20, 1975

Birthplace: Lexington, Kentucky

Instrument: **Vocals**

Favorite Musicians: Boyz II Men, Bobby Brown

Favorite Television Show: *Fresh Prince of Bel-Air*

Favorite Sport: Basketball

Favorite Color: Forest Green

Favorite Food: Macaroni and cheese

Pets: A cat named Missy

A.J.

Full Name: Alexander James McLean

Nickname: Bone

Birthday: January 9, 1978

Birthplace: West Palm Beach, Florida

Instruments: Bass, **vocals**

Favorite Musician: Barrie McKnight

Favorite Television Show: *Married...With Children*

Favorite Sport: Volleyball

Favorite Color: Purple

Favorite Food: McDonald's

Pets: A dog named Toby Wan Kenobi

Nick

Full Name: Nickolas Gene
Carter

Nickname: Nick

Birthday: January 28, 1980

Birthplace: Jamestown, New
York

Instruments: Drums, guitar,
vocals

Favorite Musicians: Oasis,
The Artist, Jodeci

Favorite Television Show:
The Simpsons

Favorite Sports: Basketball,
scuba diving

Favorite Color: Green

Favorite Food: Pizza

Pets: A dog named Boo Boo
and a cat named Pinky

Orlando Magic

In 1992, 20-year-old Kevin Richardson was singing in a local pop group in his hometown of Lexington, Kentucky. To fulfill his dream of becoming a singing star, Kevin moved to Orlando and got a job at Disney World. He appeared in park parades as the character Aladdin and as one of the Teenage Mutant Ninja Turtles.

Kevin was unhappy that he wasn't singing. A friend at work told him about three guys who had formed a singing group.

The three guys were A.J. McLean, Howie Dorough, and Nick Carter. Kevin watched them perform. He was impressed by their voices and dance moves. Kevin knew that this was the group he had been looking for.

A.J., Howie, and Nick listened to Kevin sing and watched him dance. They asked him if he wanted to be a part of their group. Kevin was very excited. The four boys decided they needed one more voice to complete the group.

They looked all over Orlando for that fifth member. They held many **auditions** but nobody seemed to fit. When they still hadn't found the voice they were looking for, Kevin came up with a great idea. He made a quick call home to his cousin Brian Littrell. Kevin knew that Brian had a great voice and the right dance moves. The very next day Brian was on a plane heading to Orlando to become the final member of the group!

The Backstreet Boys in the early days.

Naming the Band

A lot of work had to be done to start the band. The five boys had to name their group. They came up with many names but didn't like any of them. Then one day when they were at the Backstreet Market in Orlando, they thought of "Backstreet Boys." All five agreed on the name.

The next step was a bit harder. They had to choose a **manager**. Lou Pearlman, an Orlando music **producer**, heard the boys sing and knew that there was magic in their voices. He brought the boys to music managers Donna and Johnny Wright. Donna and Johnny had been very successful in the pop music business. They had managed the supergroup New Kids on the Block.

The Wrights began setting up shows for the Backstreet Boys at schools and area theme parks. Soon the Backstreet Boys became a local hit. People, especially young girls, came from all over to see them.

Word of the Backstreet Boys began to spread beyond Orlando. Soon, the Backstreet Boys had **gigs** all over Florida and even outside the state.

Clockwise from top left: Kevin, Howie, A.J., Nick, and Brian.

Jive Records

The Backstreet Boys wanted a **contract** with a record company. They auditioned for several companies, but each one turned them down. After seeing the boys play in a junior high school gym in Cleveland, Ohio, David McPherson of Jive Records saw their talent and signed the band to a contract.

Jive Records was very excited to sign the Backstreet Boys. The record company believed the boys were the next hot band. But success didn't happen overnight for the boys.

In 1995, the Backstreet Boys completed the single, "We've Got It Goin' On." The song was released in the United States and **Europe**.

The Backstreet Boys and Jive Records waited impatiently to see how well the song would do. Everyone was disappointed when the song only hit number 69 on the U.S. music charts.

The Backstreet Boys were upset that the song did not do better. But they did not give up. Although the song was not a hit in the United States, it was popular in the United Kingdom and then throughout **Europe**. The Backstreet Boys decided to go to Europe to say thanks to their fans.

The boys pose during a Jive Records photo shoot.

Crossing the Atlantic

In the summer of 1995, the Backstreet Boys toured **Europe**. They had only three songs: "We've Got It Goin' On," "I'll Never Break Your Heart," and "Roll With It." They also sang songs from their favorite singers.

Europeans loved the Backstreet Boys. Their concerts sold out and they sold thousands of albums. In December 1995, they won the *Smash Hits* Best New Tour Act award.

The Backstreet Boys' popularity spread throughout Europe. They performed TV concerts and won more awards. In January 1996, the Backstreet Boys were voted Number One International Group by viewers of Germany's television network, VIVA.

Later in 1996, the Backstreet Boys went to Canada and performed more concerts. During a concert in a Montreal shopping mall things got crazy. Thirty-five girls **collapsed** in the huge crowd. The Backstreet Boys had to be rushed out of the mall before the concert was even over! That was just the beginning.

The Backstreet Boys perform at the Vina del Mar Song Festival in Vina del Mar, Chile.

Backstreet Boys Hysteria

The Backstreet Boys sold out shows throughout **Europe** and Canada. "We've Got It Goin' On" was the number one video and song in Canada and Europe.

The Backstreet Boys couldn't go anywhere without being **mobbed**. At a radio station appearance in Germany the Backstreet Boys drew such a huge crowd that the police had to escort the group to their waiting cars.

"We've been at appearances where we have had to climb out of the windows to get out of the place because of the crowds," says Nick.

The Backstreet Boys **hysteria** was out of control. But it seemed to double when they released their first album, *Backstreet Boys*, in Europe and Canada. The record stores couldn't keep it on the shelves.

During the summer of 1996, the Backstreet Boys toured **Europe** and Canada nonstop, selling out concert after concert. They performed in Montreal in front of 70,000 screaming fans.

The Backstreet Boys toured the globe, selling out shows in Korea, Hong Kong, Japan, Malaysia, New Zealand, and Australia. They returned to Europe to tour and won MTV Europe's Viewers Choice award. They beat out Oasis and the Spice Girls.

The group returned to Canada to do 32 more shows. Each show sold out in less than 20 minutes. The Backstreet Boys was one of the hottest groups in the world. They had sold more than 11 million albums. However, they had one more country to conquer—their own.

The Backstreet Boys at a European awards show.

Backstreet's Back

In early 1997, the Backstreet Boys were happy to be home in Orlando, Florida. They had been out of the country for almost two years. The boys were determined to become a hit in the United States. They went into the recording studio and worked on new songs.

The **debut** of their first American album, also titled *Backstreet Boys*, was a major hit. The first single, "Quit Playing Games (With My Heart)," was released on June 27. Within one week it was number 24 on the charts. Within three weeks it was number one!

The Backstreet Boys were the real thing. The talented boys were now a hit throughout the world—including the United States. American magazines called the Backstreet Boys the best new group around.

The group did not forget about the countries that made them popular. The Backstreet Boys quickly released another album, *Backstreet's Back*, for their fans in Canada and **Europe**. It was a major hit.

The Backstreet Boys didn't have any time to rest. They gave interviews and performed more concerts. They made videos for both new albums, and they traveled. Although they were tired, the group couldn't have been happier. The Backstreet Boys were back.

In Charlotte, North Carolina, the Backstreet Boys kicked off a 42 city tour in 1998.

Taking A Short Break

On November 27, 1997, the Backstreet Boys were in the Macy's Thanksgiving Day Parade in New York City. Even though it was cold and the wind was blowing nearly 30 miles per hour, the Backstreet Boys climbed aboard a **float** and began singing and dancing.

Thousands of fans had waited for hours to see the Backstreet Boys in the parade. After playing for their fans, the Backstreet Boys waved good-bye and headed home to Orlando. It was time for a much needed break. The Backstreet Boys decided to take a full month off with no touring, singing, or writing.

Opposite page: The Backstreet Boys take a break from music to play in a tennis charity event.

The short break was all the Backstreet Boys needed. They were back to work one month later. The day after Christmas, they flew to Canada and started a short tour. They did 10 shows in two weeks.

After the short Canadian tour, they flew home and began working on a new album and videos. They also gave interviews for newspapers, magazines, and television shows.

They've Got It Goin' On

In 1998, the Backstreet Boys continued their **hectic** schedule. They toured the world. When it was all over, the Backstreet Boys had played in five countries and hundreds of different cities. They traveled thousands of miles and performed in front of nearly a million fans!

The Backstreet Boys did not slow down. They released their new album, *Millennium*, in May 1999. The album included many hit songs and some great videos.

Many groups try to duplicate the sound and look of the Backstreet Boys, but nobody comes close. The Backstreet Boys got it goin' on!

Opposite page: The Backstreet Boys in 1999.

Fun Facts

- A.J. sprained his ankle when he was caught in a crush of fans. He managed to perform that night with a cast on and later allowed a Montreal radio station to auction off the cast for charity.

- The Backstreet Boys have been banned from three hotels in **Europe** because their fans have gotten so out of control.

- Nick's dad had to put a fence around the family's house to keep Backstreet Boys' fans from taking clumps of grass or picking flowers as souvenirs.

The Backstreet Boys pose for a poster.

The Backstreet Boys receive the award for the World's Best-Selling Dance Group of the Year at the World Music Awards in 1998.

Glossary

audition: a short performance to test the abilities of a singer, musician, or other performer.

collapse: to fall down or cave in.

contract: an agreement between two or more parties to do or not to do something.

debut: a performer's first public appearance.

Europe: the continent between Asia and the Atlantic Ocean.

float: an exhibit carried on a car or truck in parades.

gig: a job for a performer for a specified time.

hectic: great excitement.

hysteria: an outbreak of strong emotion.

manager: a person who directs, controls, or guides someone or something.

mob: to excitedly crowd around someone or something.

producer: a person in charge of promoting a musical group, actor, or movie.

vocals: music expressed by the voice; a singer's title in a band.

Backstreet Boys on the Web

Check out the Backstreet Boys on their official Web site:

www.backstreetboys.com

Everything you ever wanted to know about the Backstreet Boys is on this awesome Web site! See the photo gallery of pictures, chat with the band or your favorite Backstreet Boy, join their fan club, get the latest news and tours, you can even shop online at the Backstreet Boys store!

Pass It On

Educate readers around the country by passing on information you've learned about your favorite young celebrity. Share your little-known facts and interesting stories. Tell others about your favorite TV shows, movies, books, and songs. We want to hear from you!

To get posted on the ABDO Publishing Company Web site, email us at "youngprofiles@abdopub.com"
Visit the ABDO Publishing Company Web site at www.abdopub.com

Index